Forbidden Fruit

Poems of Love, Loss, Hope and Regret

Brandy L Prettyman

Indigo Quill Publications
Papillion, NE

Forbidden Fruit
Poems of Love, Loss, Hope and Regret

Copyright © 2020
Prettyman Holdings LLC

All rights reserved. No part of this book may be reproduced or transmitted in any form or by any means, including but not limited to information storage and retrieval systems, electronic, mechanical, photocopy, recording, etc. without written permission from the copyright holder.

ISBN-13: 978-0-9980904-5-0 (paperback)
ISBN-13: 978-0-9980904-8-1 (ebook)

Library of Congress Control Number: 2020923757

Photography by Meghan Nichole Robertson
Other images from Adobe Stock
Edited and designed by Julie Haase (www.copysitter.com)

Published by
Indigo Quill Publications
Papillion, NE

First Edition, First Printing

To Terry

Your life was not nearly long enough, but the time we spent together shaped me in ways I am still learning.

Contents

Acknowledgments vii
Author's Note ix

A Note 1
The First Day 2
New Beginnings 4
Reunion Delayed 5
Life's Illusion 6
Together Apart 8
Torn Map 10
Evolution 11
Kolkata 12
Winds of Change 15
Those Left Behind 16
The Ghost 18
Day 821 19
Oh, to Be a Star! 22
Lust's Regret 23
Ocean Vacation 24
New Love 25
Soul Thief 26
A Sister's Call 28
Living in the Past 29
The Night Has No Answers 30
Secret Keeper 32
Madness 33
Hell's Angels 34
Escape 35
Determination in the Face of Doubt 36
Delicate Balance 39
Our Quest 40
Desire 42

About the Author 45

Acknowledgments

So many people believe writing is something done alone, a solitary pasttime (because honestly, who really makes it a career?) that is held together by the frantic mumblings of the crazed creators with a gift for stringing together letters and syllables into something more than the words formed. But in truth, writing is a community. Every good writer has someone to thank. Every great writer has a tribe. A society of individuals, putting forward their support to raise up a writer to greatness.

My little hamlet includes so many who made this publication possible. Each provided something concrete—whether they knew or understood what they offered was more than just words of encouragement but a lifeline to make mistakes and learn from them along the way.

I cannot acknowledge my success without tipping my hat to the group that accepted me all those years ago and has let me gain confidence in my craft. "Chuck," as we lovingly call ourselves, is a ragtag bunch with linguistic loves as diverse as the people that make up our merry band of writers and poets. They have suffered through some truly terrible writing of mine and helped me hone this craft into something I am proud of.

A big thanks to the Nebraska Writers Guild. Though they may not know it, Guild publications have allowed me not only the thrill of acceptance and having an audience but the harsh lessons that come from literary rejection as well. I received my first publishing credentials in an NWG anthology, and I am grateful for the opportunity to be a part of a literary community greater than myself.

I must take a moment to thank the hard work and dedication of Julie Haase, my designer, editor, and all around badass, and Charlene Pierce for her helpful (and thoughtful) feedback.

Last but certainly not least, my family. They have listened to me read and have watched me write poetry, most of which they did not want to do but did so because that is what family does. They encourage you to go out on a limb, to embrace your dreams and pursue your passions. They may not understand your goals, but they give you the space to test out your wings and learn to fly.

Specifically to my husband: Thank you for giving me the space to concentrate on writing. Your support through this journey has been incalculable.

For my children: Your antics and love have given me years of material to sift through. Your interactions with each other and with the world around you inform how I see the world. You are each an inspiration.

With Love,
~ B

Author's Note

The work contained within is a work from the heart of the poet but not without angst, anguish, fear, and doubt.

The words and emotions are raw, perhaps too raw for those currently walking with new grief. The following pages include topics of adultery, incest, abandonment, anxiety, self-harm, and death, among others.

A Note

My writing—so personal
but not always true.

It is the emotion of the moment,
a story played out on the page.

The prose is not meant to be prophetic
or historical but self-healing.

To remove the negative, odd or unworthy
from my mind to the page—where it is safe.

Where it can be
viewed,
studied,
understood.
Destroyed
after autopsy.
Allowing my mind
to explore the taboo
without being engulfed
and absorbed
into the abyss.

The First Day

The gown flowed around her.
The satin cascading down her hips
as she danced in time to the music, waiting.

A samba played, his favorite.
Her dancing was a prelude
to his arrival in an open-breasted suit,
ready to sweep her off her feet.

Excitement and elation were written
on her face as she watched her love
move toward her with a swagger in his step
and a smile in his eyes.

His tall, straight back carried him closer
until his sexy smile was close enough
to melt her heart and set her on fire.

He reached out and grabbed her hand.
Holding it, enveloping it with his own and
surrounding her with his love and warmth.
A slight tug, commanding their first dance
to begin as husband and wife.

As he gathered her close in his arms, the guests
watched their love unfold on the stage.
She cast her gaze up to his.
His height, not towering but protective,
Left her heart glowing
with wonder and wanting.
He smiled down at her.
His own eyes filled with desire.

She blushed and glanced away.
A shy smile on her face. He spun her around,
through friends and family.

Their love showcased for all those present.
Witnesses to the victory of love.
Their journey, just beginning.

She looked back up to his face
but his eyes have changed.
They have become colder, lacking the warmth
that made her fall for him.

Before her eyes he is gone.
Her hand now held, not lovingly in his,
but by the tangled sheets
where he once lay and will never lie again.

New Beginnings

The purple tinged sky
overlooked the calm waters
that gently lapped against the shore.

Your sweet breath
washed over my face
as your lips sang above mine.

On that Indian Summer night
we found sweet innocence
in the loving arms of a stranger.

In the grey light of dawn
you caressed my body
as a poet caresses a sigh.

We parted ways
before the light of day
spilled across the horizon.

You walked to the east,
I to the south,
as the gentle waters of the lake
sang us a song.

Reunion Delayed

The ocean rushes to meet the shore.
Desperate to feel the warm brown sand,
anxious to become one with itself again.
Ready to pull its two halves back to whole.

The shore refuses to give in, to give up.
It protests every wave
lapping lazy against its sand.
Determined to live its own life,
ignoring the siren cry of home.

Life's Illusion

The box mocks me,
broken and torn,
from all my attempts to create it.
Brazen in its defiance of my desire.
All I want is a sturdy box.
My tears fall as I sit
and take in my not-so-handy work.

The bottom is askew,
cardboard refusing to bend to *my* will,
instead following the slanted folds
ingrained at what should be the edge,
leaving a gap where the flaps do not meet.

Tape hanging from the mangled end,
laughing as it watches me try.
A metaphor for my new life
where nothing *listens*
and everything mocks me.

A life I have begun to pack away,
one misshapen box at a time,
over the last month
of bitterness and betrayal.

Determined, in spite of the pain,
a testament to my resilience
as I watch my life torn apart
by one too many lies.

My fractured future tainted
by the cries of "what if"

that find solace in my mind;
unspoken scenarios haunt me.
I am unable to break free
from the weight of the past.

They are hard,
the truths I don't want to face.
The life I thought we were living
was just a mirage,
an illusion of truth
you allowed me to believe
until four weeks ago
when the illusion lost its luster.
Your new love gave you an ultimatum:
Her or Me.

Twenty-nine days of slow acceptance.
What I knew was not truth at all.
I believed the pretty lies you spread,

the illusion of our life.

I still fight against my new truth;
in the dark of night I let those
"what ifs" out of their home in my mind
and let them roam freely in ~~our~~ my home.

But I pack them away in the early light of dawn
when they have less hold over me.
When the light shines on my worth
and lets me believe in the hope
of tomorrow.

Together Apart

The garden of succulents
on the window ledge table
watch me.
They see me take in a new world through
the 32" Vizio TV screen now doubling
as my computer monitor

My own window to a world
I can no longer be a full member of,
a world now separated by six feet
of social distancing

A window that has shown my parents
are not infallible;
they are human.
They will post things
for the world to see,
things I would never
have imagined them saying
in the company of others.
The vitriol of someone who
for far too long has felt their own voice
was not heard.

My monitor is now a doorway
to social gatherings with friends
who drink their alcohol together on Zoom
but alone in their homes.

It is a portal that shows me
the greatness I have achieved
in spite of the state of the world
trying to kill us all off one by one.

The apps tracking
the weight I have lost,
and gained back,
but in fairness I lost it once
and can do so again
when the insanity of our divisions
has been healed with
communication and an understanding
different does not mean wrong.

Torn Map

I am in no position to judge or council
I have done things
I never thought I would dare
I have seen things
I never thought possible
I am not who I thought I was
nor am I who I always dreamed I would be

My compass is broken; I have lost my way
My station in this world as a woman is
my only contribution to this damaged place
My only solace in my past deeds
is my ability to forget and leave them
silent in the past

I am only human
Flesh and bone, saint and sinner
My moral high ground washed away leaving
only a torn map of the murky road
upon which we all travel.

Evolution

Dust drifting within the beam of sunshine
Dancing, quiet, peaceful, still
Small particles of our home intertwine

The home we built, my location, your design
Our surprise getaway, the suspense, the thrill
Dust drifting within the beam of sunshine

Your framed print of the New York skyline
My Broadway swag, a cast-signed handbill
Small particles of our home intertwine

Business meetings that ran late, clandestine
Your gaze on the neighbor from our windowsill
Dust drifting within the beam of sunshine

The lipstick red on your collar, not mine
My hotel receipt from Charlottesville
Small particles of our home intertwine

Two children born—each form a new bloodline
The vows we spoke, unable to fulfill
Dust drifting within the beam of sunshine
Small particles of our home intertwine

Kolkata

On the streets of Kolkata
a man sits alone.
Reading
from a book with no pages,
spewing forth filth
and golden knowledge alike.

I passed by this man
in tattered clothes one day.
Amazed at his brazenness,
I asked from what book he read.
His answer chilled me to the core.

With dark, soulless eyes
he stared straight through me.
Then focused on my being,
proclaimed to be reading
my past, my present, my future.

I thought,
surely this man is a huckster
looking for quick coin.
He will say these broad,
meaningless phrases
that say all and nothing
within the same breath

But as he peered at my torso,
he began to recite
the actions of my life.
As if that pageless book
contained my soul
and all the knowledge it holds.

He told me
of my heartaches,
my joys,
my loves,
my losses.

He told me
of the journey that led me
to stand before him now.
He recited the path I had already planned
to take on my way from the City.

His eyes lost focus.
"You will find your fate on the winding road."
He turned away
finished with his prophecy,
finished with me.

Down the streets of Kolkata
I began to wander
following my plan
and his prophecy of my future.

An endless search for the Fate
prophesied by a man reading
from an empty book
began that same day.
In everything seen,
in everything tasted,
in everything touched.

Years after I passed through that City,
with the arrogance of youth

and the ignorance of the unlearned,
I finally recognized
the unspoken meaning of his words.

In searching for my fate
prophesied by a man I did not know
I had missed the life Fate
had placed in front of my eyes.

Winds of Change

A breeze blows, harsh and cold
smelling of time long past.
It tastes of regret and words never said,
of people never loved and a life never lived

I stand alone, shivering
taking in the terror.
I may never be given the opportunity
to correct the mistakes of my youth.

The sun peeks out
from behind the gray clouds
shining down a warm hope
of a time soon to come.

Faith in renewal and hope of what could be.
Faith in my future possibilities.
The promise a past does not dictate
the path of destiny.

I revel in the glow of the dappled sunlight
as it drapes over my skin
promising better days to come
if I can only let go of yesterday.

Those Left Behind

I cannot remember the faces
of those left behind.
Nor can I see the agony
etched into their skin,
making its way
from inside to out.

What I will never forget,
what has been seared
into my consciousness,
are the sounds.

The intonation of the officiant,
quiet and strong,
introducing those closest
as they approach the lectern
to remind us of those lost.

Who they were, what they did, how they loved.

The melody of song,
voices straining through tears,
voices raised high
to lift the spirit
of both the dead and those remaining.

The poignant cries
echo in my mind.

Forceful

Mournful

Life Altering

Sounds that express
grief more accurately than words.
Heartbreaking sobs that
shatter the quiet air.

Death has taken another victim.

The Ghost

Trust is an apparition.

A specter
integral to our everyday
dancing on the periphery of our lives.

Appreciated
only when its ghostly fingers
are no longer present.

An illusion
granting us one brief moment
when we can forget we are human
and prone to heartbreak.

Day 821

Moonlight cascades over
my devastated face
as you turn away
from Us.

The soft light is filtered
through the bay window
tinted grayish-blue.

The window film applied
with gentle but impatient hands,
ready to be done with the project.
There are gaps at the edges.

Sinking to the floor
I let the memories
envelop me,
caress me,
hold me,
so I do not shatter.

The images
of a life lived,
a family created,
a world all our own,
repeat through in my mind.

The new desk purchased
that didn't quite fit
through the doorway.

The flowers you would buy
and leave on the desk you built

for me after the one we bought
was returned.

You walk out the front door,
the one we just painted last year,
the quiet closing echoes
like a bomb.

An explosion
of words you never said,
of things you kept hidden,
of your final words.

I listen, dazed,
as you drive from our home
for the last time.
I pick myself up
but I can't say how long
I sat there, numb . . .

It has been more than two years
Since that fateful night
You told me you loved me
But were no longer in love.

There are days
I must still remind myself
this room is no longer ours
But is instead mine.

I have changed so much.
A new desk now resides
where your desk for me,
built with loving hands,
used to sit.

It finally reflects me.
A new space to embrace the creative
and ignore the past heartbreak
peeking through cracks
between the window's tint and edge.

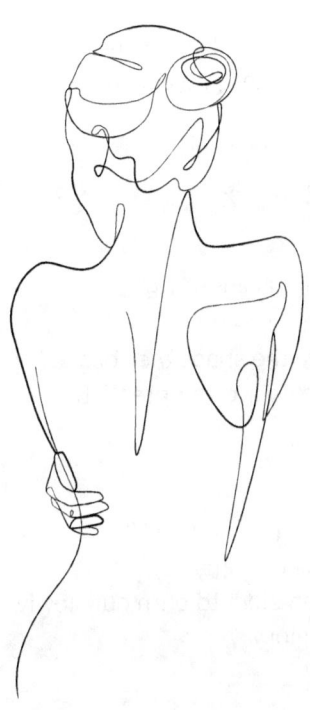

Oh, to Be a Star!

The stars play hopscotch in the sky.
Gregarious
leaping, breezing through their lives,
living as if this millennium may be their last.

Oh, to be a star!

Enveloped
in the tranquil sea of inky blackness
Calling out to a mate lightyears away.
Your core lighting up
when they twinkle in return;
a bond unlike any other.

Comforted
by a universe filled with those
bigger and grander,
knowing despite the space *they* occupy
you will still live your own potential,
your own story.

Fated
to be the vessel of a child's wish,
to hold the hope of humanity.
Knowing you can elect to burn out slowly
or flame out in glory.

Lust's Regret

It began with a look which led to a caress.
It ended with a shift of my known universe.

An imperceivable movement
most will never feel and
some will never understand.
Certainly no one will approve.

Falling
to pieces

Falling
in love

Falling
from grace

A placeholder, not my replacement
but the turning of a page
that can never be undone.

Bathed in gentle light we stand at an impasse.
Your smile does not reach your eyes.
Regret taints the air between us.

Ocean Vacation

The rush of water
flows in his mouth,
filling his lungs,
delivering his final thoughts
of today.

New Love

I am a sucker for tall men.
Broad shoulders to cry on,
wide arms to hold me
in comfort, in passion.

Bare, chiseled cheeks
lay gentle on my head.
The perfect difference in height
to be enveloped in an embrace.

With blue eyes that have this way
of stopping my breath and
catching me against my will.
Holding me hostage with a cerulean gaze.

He must have a good laugh,
Gregarious and boastful,
Excited to share joy with everyone
if they want to listen or not.

A man that can stare into my eyes,
speaking without words,
can lead me anywhere with
strong hands that engulf my own.

Soul Thief

Every day feels
as if I am walking
through a cotton haze.
The thick air suffocating me,
stealing the breath
from my lungs.
Eyelids heavy—
almost impossible to raise
over sorrow-filled eyes.

They say Time
heals all wounds.
I wonder how They know
what Time will do,
whoever They are.

How will Time
affix me to the fading shore
with my mooring gone?
How can Time fill the void?
Repair the hole in my heart
where he once lived?

Will Time create another
to replace what was lost?
Fill the gaping space
where my heart once beat?

Will Time
stop replaying
the best years of my life
I will never again experience

and release me from the prison
that holds me captive?

Or will Time,
that fickle Soul Thief,
leave me to rot in my cell and
force upon me the cruel laughter
of the devil that taunts me
with love's lost memory?

A Sister's Call

A line of light
shines through my window
as thoughts flutter through my mind.

Morning again.

She shall never again
see the light of day
through human eyes.

Her feet no longer touch the floor.
Her spirit calls to me
this sunny morning,
bridging a gaping hole
between reality and spirituality.

I am mourning again.

Waiting for midnight to come
to take my pain away
until it is morning again.

Living in the Past

I am torn.

Between this life
and the life I left behind,
Between what I have now
and what I will now never have.

I am fractured.

One decision so easy to make then,
when there was no other choice,
haunts my dreams.
The chance of change seeps
into my subconscious where it plays,
tricks my mind
every day since that day.

I am broken.

Like bone against concrete.
The faint sounds of laughter
that never will be,
the small hand curled so tightly in mine
that will only exist
in my mind's eye.

The Night Has No Answers

I watch you approach
your eyes burning with desire.
A hand reaches out; I am paralyzed where I lie.

Touching, feeling.

Your hand presses to my body. Lips to flesh.
You continue your journey
until you can wait no longer.
The scent of desire fills the room.

You finish what you came here to start
as my silent tears fall to the floor.
You leave as quietly as you came
but your presence still lingers.
Hours after you've gone
I still feel your hands moving over my body.

I shiver at the thought.

The tears come freely now
as if a dam has broken
inside my wounded heart.
The moonlight shines down upon my face and
I whisper the forbidden question into the night . . .

Why, Daddy?

Secret Keeper

Darkness has fallen
I feel cold in sunshine
Alone in a crowd
The secrets I intended to keep
Now keep me
They have locked me in a prison
Of invisible walls
Walls that only Help can break through
I scream for Help to come
But it never does
The walls remain firm
For my secret keeps me

Madness

Alone in the crowded space
I am screaming
with an empty voice.
People pass me with only a glance,
blind to my torment,
my fear,
ignorant of the torturous tricks
played and perpetuated
by my very own mind.

I now find myself
sitting in a gnat-infested room,
silence my only company.
The crowds have left but
the eyes in the walls follow
my every move
silently condemning me,
my very existence,
to that of a forgotten memory.

Hell's Angels

Angelic faces stare back at me
through the glass pane that houses them
recrimination burning in their sweet eyes.

The soft, heavenly voices drift through
pleading with me to change my mind
and turn around before it's too late.

But those cherubic voices only come
after the damage is done.
Only now as I peer into those trusting orbs
do I hear their cries.
Too late to ease their fears,
far too gone to comfort them now.

The decision is made.
The die has been cast.
The life that once was is no more.
And just like those storied men of the King's,
no amount of trying will put us together again.

Escape

Dust swirled
hot and dry
as an over-sized moon
hung in the sky.

Testing, teasing,
torturing my mind.
Reflecting the flames from behind me

A singular thought
dances through my consciousness,
"How could you?"
As I glance back, swift,
to watch the destruction I have wrought
by the simple act of walking away.

The house
still there
still burning
seems to call out to me
"Don't leave."

Or is it the call of my lover?
Gentle, Deceitful, Bruising.
Begging me to stay
while he burns our lives to the ground.

Determination in the Face of Doubt

Banking to the left
the horizon disappears under the wing.
All I can see are cloudy skies
bathed in dappled sunlight.
Signaling hope.

We even out and the surface of the earth
comes rushing into view once more.
A stark reminder.
Clouds obscure patches of the ground
as we begin our descent
then disappear again leaving
cars that no longer look like toys,
buildings no longer blocks on a carpeted floor.

Instead they grow just as my anxiety grows
the closer we come to real life.
I have hidden from that life,
waiting for the pain to subside,
waiting for a sign—one I can embrace,
hold as I march forward without breaking.

But it does not appear.
There is no hiding from the truth.
I must face the hurt and the anguish
I have caused because of my betrayal.

The phone in the seat back, once dark,
now alights with missed calls and texts.
My abandonment of my duties, my promises,

flash over and over and over.
Reminders.

I face a choice as I wait to leave
the safe haven this plane has become.
I have never been erratic, always the one
To hold everyone together
even as I break apart.
Now, after the erratic behavior of the past
hours,
I must decide.

Phone in hand, I exit the plane.
A new city with no trace of my past,
a new passport created with a new name.
The offending phone, blinking, buzzing.
A reminder of my past
I no longer wish to carry.

I sit at a nondescript restaurant,
strangers to my left and right,
and order a $12 drink that I will pay for
with cash I have taken from our joint account.

The phone begins to jump on the table,
buzzing again in anger from your
unanswered attempts to find out where I am.

I put the phone on silent,
begin the factory reset while I sip my drink.

I pull the back cover from my last connection
to a life I no longer want,
take the battery out and remove the SIM card.
I leave the phone, toss the battery
and pocket the SIM.
I have made up my mind.

This is a stopover only—a hub for the airline.
I make my way to the baggage claim
to retrieve my small case.
Back up to ticketing,
where I pay for my ticket to freedom
with my new passport and our old money.

Delicate Balance

The water has long since grown cold.

Frigid

The scars had long ago healed, physically.

It had been years since she had the thoughts.
Thoughts such as those that plagued her now.
Years since the only relief she could find
was beneath a short razor blade

And yet

Here she sits,
blade delicately balanced
between finger and thumb,
her most recent Mother's Day present
glittering on her ring finger.

The demons had returned in full force,
driving her to the point
of no return.

Our Quest

Where human meets nature
a place of unnatural beauty exists.
I gaze down the shoreline
enchanted by the image
superimposed
upon the image in my mind.

Each on opposite ends
of this glorious curve of sand,
both making our way
back to the middle.

I realize our journey
along this stretch of coastline
mirrors that of our own lives.

You
so anxious to get to "The Next,"
quick and decisive,
you make a decision
and run to the outcome.

I
plodding with definitive, methodical steps,
moving at my own pace,
more akin to the sea turtle
than the wave.

Neither is wrong.
Neither is better.
Just different.

We embark on our own journeys
using different means, different strengths
to reach the same destination.

Desire

The firelight caresses your face
Your silhouette glows gold
And matches the glass of champagne
That sparkles in your hand

Delight bubbles through my soul
Knowing I have finally found
What I thought I would never have

A sweet berry dipped in chocolate
Brushes my lips
Then it is gone, replaced by something
So much sweeter

Your kiss burns my lips
As you begin the journey
Through the field of my body

Exploring what you have known for so long
Yet finding what you never saw before

"The First Day" was originally published in *Voices from the Plains, Volume III* by the Nebraska Writers Guild.

"Evolution" was originally published in *How It Looks from Here: Poetry from the Plains* by the Nebraska Writers Guild.

About the Author

Brandy L Prettyman is a writer, singer, painter, mother, wife, Army veteran, and coffee snob.

A professional jack-of-all-trades, Brandy has earned a Bachelor in Business Administration and spent the last decade (maybe it's longer, but let's not make this awkward) reading and writing poetry as well as working on a debut novel. She enjoys delving deeper into her chosen profession by attending conventions for authors, and sometimes is asked to present classes at those same conventions on writing believable dialogue.

Brandy has been published in multiple anthologies, including the Nebraska Writers Guild poetry collection *How it Looks from Here: Poetry from the Plains* and literary anthologies *Voices from the Plains, Volume III* and *Voices from the Plains, Volume IV*. Her writing tends to explore the dark emotions we face when confronted by our own morality and mortality. If you are interested in her day-to-day ramblings, visit her at her blog: The Journey Journal (www.brandyprettyman.com/journeyjournal).

Brandy lives and works from home in Papillion, Nebraska, and spends her spare time traveling the world with her three kids (when they are home) and her husband. Most days she can be found drinking a large latte at her writing desk, frantically writing her thoughts down in verse before they disappear.

www.ingramcontent.com/pod-product-compliance
Lightning Source LLC
Chambersburg PA
CBHW070441010526
44118CB00014B/2138